MANAGEMENT BITES II

A BROAD BACKGROUND IN RECRUITING AND HUMAN RESOURCES GIVES ME A CLEAR PICTURE OF WHY AND HOW PEOPLE RISE TO THE TOP.

THIS BOOK IS WRITTEN FOR NEW SUPERVISORS, NEW MANAGERS LOOKING FOR FUTURE SUCCESS.

LEADERSHIP CAN BE AN INNATE TALENT OR LEARNED.

WHETHER YOU HAVE JUST BEEN PROMOTED OR TAKEN ON YOUR FIRST MANAGEMENT POSITION, THIS BOOK IS DIRECTED TO YOU AND TO YOUR FUTURE.

DECIDE IF YOU WANT TO BE A TOP MANAGER, CEO, OR AN 'A' LIST MANAGER.

Table of contents

CHAPTER I

FIRST SUPERVISORY / MANAGEMENT JOB

Congratulations! You have just been promoted into your first supervisory or junior managerial position. This is the beginning of a career. This is the time to grow and learn.

Ask yourself these questions:

> **Do you know why you were selected?**
>
> **What do you know about supervising others?**
>
> **Do you know how to motivate a team?**

Do you have a background in a school setting or elsewhere that gives you insight into motivating a team?

> **As you go into this first level of executive positions, you need to analyze, and to think before you act.**

When first put in this position, it usually means more money, and more responsibility. The drawback is that many people are so self absorbed, that they fail to understand that one now becomes more vulnerable. To succeed your mission must be understood, as well as the reasons for the promotion.

This is a discussion you need to have with the "powers that be". Some possibilities: technical ability, team orientation or great personality.

Having been involved in career creation at various stages, upper management's decision-making process fascinated me. Sometimes, one individual could simply make a habit of flattering the boss, and achieve great success. It is one way to get ahead. It does not particularly guarantee success or longevity, but it still can work.

Within the Human Resources function, it was my job to validate promotions. One sure way to do it, was to question the people now reporting to that person, and also ask for input from departments with regular interaction.

Here is a general list of questions:

On a scale of 1 – 5 (5 being the best) rate candidates in these skills:

> Technical ability
> Communicates clearly and constructively
> Able to train effectively
> Approaches problems creatively
> Team player
> Self motivated
> Reacts well to pressure
> Meets deadlines
> Follows up until job is done.

A Human Resources professional's contribution to the success of any organization, is the core value of that position. The mission never varies:

LESSON: **Get and keep the best people.**

Once, when my boss needed a secretary, I recommended mine. He was reluctant, because although very efficient, she was extremely shy. However, I knew her capabilities and convinced him to try her out for two weeks. If at the end he was not interested then she could return to me. He begrudgingly agreed. In the meantime, I advertised and interviewed for an administrative assistant so no time would be lost.

After two weeks, this Manager realized that this young woman was excellent. I could not have gotten her back. In the interim, I had developed candidates for the existing gap.

LESSON: **Give people a chance to move up.**

In another hotel, a great waiter was offered a promotion to Host, or Assistant Manager. He was reluctant to change. Management agreed to give him 30 days in the position and see if he and they would like it. After 30 days, he wanted to return to being a server.

LESSON: **Don't push people into jobs that don't interest them, regardless of the reason.**

Success comes with a certain love for your job, or your co-workers or the people you serve. Dishwashers and housemen on a property care very much about the person they report to and with whom they work. Finding a reliable crew to work in areas demanding low skills can make an organization strong.

It is important for management and non-management personnel to understand that "chemistry" and personality are part of the hiring equation.

I've seen technically proficient people put in charge of major projects because of their intelligence, education and skill. Even though deemed the smartest, they often cannot manage others. As you rise in your profession, you need to learn the art of motivation and delegation. Ascending the pyramid means more responsibility and the ability to know what, when and how to delegate. In a science project, expertise is required and an understanding of the ultimate goal.

How do you engage the interest and attention of the people you supervise? How do you convince those who report to you, to act in the best interests of the project and of the organization?

When you deal with those who promoted you, ask what they see in your background that prompted the decision.

- What do they see as the biggest challenge?
- Who else was interviewed for the job?
- What was the main reason he/she failed to receive the position?
- What do you have to do to be star?
- What tools do you need from them?
- What time lines exist?

CHAPTER II

DISCUSSIONS WITH YOUR IMMEDIATE BOSS

New on the job or just promoted? Regardless -- know your boss's priorities. Do not try to guess. **ASK.**

Pick a good time to approach your boss to set up a meeting. Tell the truth. "I'm interested in knowing your thoughts on the goals for the department and for me."

If there's any reluctance or hesitation on his/her part, simply state that "Working for the success of the company, the department and myself, makes it crucial that we talk. I would appreciate at least 15 minutes of your time to start. That way we can work together to set up near term and future goals."

THE MEETING: Your first question might be "Give me your definition of this department's success". What will it look like?

If you were promoted within the department where you worked, ask why that decision was made. Do not assume anything.

If anyone else in the department was considered for this job, what type of resentment could I face?

What in my experience, do you see as most valuable to this operation? Where do you think I might need help?

What do you see as your biggest challenge and mine?

NEXT STEP

Plan to interview everyone reporting to you to understand individual career goals. How will you be able to help them? This may mean offering more training. Will that be a problem?

Keep in mind that if you lack mastery in certain areas, you will need to achieve it. Even a mediocre effort can bring you insight into what talent individual positions require.

Work assignments are easier to make when a department head or manager understands how each task is accomplished.

CHAPTER III

GET TO KNOW YOUR STAFF

As a new manager, you need to know what motivates each member of your staff. Leading any group requires attention to detail. Knowing what type of personalities you are supervising is vital.

Start a private discussion with each person with no interruptions. A sampling of questions could include:

- What do you think is your major contribution to our operations?
- Is there any area that you prefer over another?
- What are your career goals?
- What kind of training would interest you?
- If you were in charge of this project/department, what would you do first?
- What do you think is the biggest challenge facing this team/company?
- Have you set goals for the year, month?

Personal information is necessary to evaluate time and commitment issues. Learn the extent of life commitments.

- Tell me a bit about what brought you into this industry?
- What was your major in College? Or have you ever wanted to attend college?
- Find out about family relationships, the success or lack thereof of the parents.
- Married or single? Children – ages – What does your spouse do for a living?
- What do you do in your spare time?

Truly get to know your staff. Ask how they like to be managed. If you manage differently, speak up. Establish an on-going dialogue with your crew.

The old days of leading by fear or because of your position are gone. Smart people want to be challenged. To succeed, you need an intelligent group around you willing to share ideas.

Also in general, young people do their best work when given a chance to shine. If you have an older staff, find out what they like doing and have them participate in training others.

KEY: MAKE GOOD USE OF THE TALENT AROUND YOU.

LEARN TO GIVE CREDIT WHERE CREDIT IS DUE!

CHAPTER IV

TEAM SELECTION

A budget dictates the number of your staff. In my experience within the Human Resources function, the size of the staff is related to the number of open positions and turnover.

In a hotel, the pre-opening HR staff can be large. Usually in that instance I would have either trainees or part timers working for me: The trainees were dispersed to other parts of the hotel, as the HR needs dwindled.

HR offices always call for detail oriented and out going people. After opening over 19 hotels from scratch, I have found ways to advertise and to sift through thousands of resumes in an expeditious manner.

Pre-opening the key managers are the first to be identified. A large company will transfer or promote a certain amount of people into these positions and look outside for some new talent.

As a matter of experience, it became clear that no one should be promoted into a major position during an opening.

This is the time for very competent leaders to be in charge. Nothing goes as planned and therefore the more seasoned executives have the edge. They adapt quickly, can change plans, take a new direction and move ahead with confidence. This is hard to do unless you are thoroughly trained or familiar with a job.

To avoid **mass hiring** and its inevitable stresses, I fostered the idea of interviewing for all positions well in advance. Candidates were evaluated, references checked and all information put into each department's file.

When the department head arrives, interviews can be set up and applicants approved for hire with all paper work done months or weeks in advance. The future employee is given a tentative start date and told that if that changes he/she will be notified at least two weeks in advance: enough time to give notice. This way if someone does not come for orientation, we simply rip up the paper work.

When this idea was challenged at the corporate level, they predicted no one would show up. Out of 300 + staff, only one person failed to appear.

Team selection calls for job descriptions, and understanding the supervisor's management style. To lessen turnover, evaluate a candidate's potential with the company.

I often took on bright, attractive applicants with limited English skills as dishwashers, knowing that once their command of the language solidified, they might qualify for cocktail or restaurant servers, or move into housekeeping and become supervisors. The key component even for "back of the house" is energy, with a willingness and interest in serving the public.

In selecting staff for Human Resources, my choice is people who enjoy dealing with a diverse group of nationalities. Many hotels employees come from different countries. Working in HR also requires a very calm disposition and the willingness to deal with constant interruptions.

The paper work is voluminous and people issues are always part of the daily scene.

HR REPRESENTS MANAGEMENT.

This means that every employee must be recognized and listened to. The Human Resources mission should always be to get and keep the best people.

To succeed, management needs to understand the concerns of all staff.

CHAPTER V

INTERVIEWING

Strong leaders know who and what skills their team needs to succeed.

Interviewing skill is crucial in a leadership role.

No one person can do it all. Supervisors and managers must know how to motivate a team.

Dynamic leaders seek the best people available.

The goal is to know what skills are needed to run a project or a department. Know the type of talent that will complement yours, not mirror it. Look to the past. When and where did you operate with the best staff? What elements created successful teamwork? Know exactly the type of personalities you want on your team. Hiring "Yes" people is perilous.

CREATE A JOB DESCRIPTION

- Why does this position exist?
- What skills are a must?
- What skills are desirable but not essential?
- What must be accomplished on a regular basis?
- What tasks call for specific time frames or deadlines?
- What type of education or equivalent experience is needed?
- What are physical requirements of the job?
- What is the minimum amount of experience needed.

YOUR GOAL IS TO GET AND KEEP THE BEST PEOPLE.

CREATE A DIALOGUE

Start in a private place with no interruptions.

First interview should be with only one person. Create a comfortable space, so the individual answers your questions fluidly, candidly. You are there to decide if this job is the right match for the person, as well as the company.

Look at body language. Is a sense of energy projected? How does this person greet you? Does the prospect make eye contact, with a firm handshake, and good posture? Is the interviewee professionally dressed? If a non-management position, the attire still needs to convey a sense of neatness.

Watch how the person sits in a chair. Do they sit down before you ask them or do they just take a chair of their own choice. Do they lean back (too relaxed) or lean forward (too nervous). Are they graceful or clumsy? Do they have nervous habits: shaking a foot, tapping on an arm rest?

Too much jewelry, cologne, make-up or shoes not shined? These things count even in menial jobs. Even when hiring unskilled workers, a clean appearance and good manners are crucial.

Everyone in an organization deals with others, unless they are locked in a laboratory. Employees that work together easily are an asset and strengthen a company. Particularly at the unskilled levels, the staff cares deeply about their team.

QUESTIONS

Tell me about yourself.

See what the person emphasizes. What do they talk about? Do they have a pre-prepared narrative? A seasoned executive should be able to answer this succinctly in less than 3 minutes. Someone at a less skilled level, will usually tell you a personal story. Listen carefully. Whatever is key to the story is a major part of the individual's psyche and character.

Tell me about the best/worst boss you ever had?

Describe the character traits of the person?

What type of job has brought the most satisfaction?

Tell me about your biggest disappointment at work?
- Would you have done anything differently?
- Did this happen because of outside circumstances?
- Had you contributed to the issue?
- What was the end result?

Analyze the information

Will the job for which you are recruiting be the right one for the candidate?
You are looking to learn an individual's motivation and driving force. Where will they thrive?

Using Sports as an analogy here are some considerations.

Physically can a person do the job? For example: you are probably not going to consider someone 5' 2" for your basketball team or a blind person for your Pitcher or Catcher.

If a job requires physical strength and energy, those qualities need to be part of the job description.

Intellectual ability: Accounting, or computer work requires an ability to handle numbers, to present technical data, and to be detail oriented. A test would be appropriate.

Guest contact or dealing with the public: an interest in dealing with the public. Pleasant personality and a calm disposition are essential.

Attention to detail. Almost every position requires some ability to be good with figures, filing and checking.

KNOW WHAT YOU WANT AND NEED. Have a clear idea of the critical qualities required.

When looking for an administrative type, call on the phone first. Does the individual know how to deal with business spontaneously? Is natural courtesy obvious? You know that most call centers are in the Midwest where regional accents are clear and where there is a reputation for good manners and helpfulness -- community spirit.

Look at superficial elements first. A resume with job after job in perhaps a 1 to 3-year period is not a good sign but can be a telephone question. This type of instability or no specific path of increasing responsibilities indicates either a bland work environment with no opportunity to learn, no personal ambition or perhaps limited intelligence. Smart people need and seek challenges. Not every job requires a smart person.

Labor intensive jobs such as bellman, doorman, truck driver, dishwasher, cleaner are positions that call for persistence, consistency, and a good work ethic more than education.

Dynamic Leaders need to have the best people. The goal is to know what skills are needed to run a project or a department. Look for the type of talent that will complement, not mirror, yours.

Look to the past. When and where did you operate with the best staff? What elements created teamwork? Know exactly the type of personalities you want on your team. Ask the right questions; evaluate the answers and the body language. Listen carefully and observe.

Leadership is evident when the mission and philosophy of an operation is shared and understood by all. Whether the manager is present or not, everyone knows what to do.

CHAPTER VI

LISTENING

This skill is the one most often lacking in people.

As a teenager, I went to live in Italy with just basic skills in Italian. It amazed me how many people praised me as a wonderful conversationalist. In fact, I was listening very carefully trying to understand what was being said. When this happened I often nodded and once in a while, would say very expressively "No, non e vero!" translation: No, it can't be true". Sometimes I would use " Si." (yes) or "davero" (really). The joke was that I had the perfect accent without the slightest Italian.

The first rule of listening is to pay attention and by nodding, and minor comments, keep the conversation flowing.

Because confrontation can be difficult, I developed a way of asking questions that gave me information and also a chance to paraphrase what had been said. Done in a non-threatening manner, individuals can often see where they have been unreasonable or hyperbolic.

Example: A young night chef and a room service cashier got into a heated argument in the kitchen and both were suspended from the floor. The next day they were in my office together.

I asked first one and then the other to explain what happened with no interruptions allowed.

Listening carefully it became clear that the cashier provoked the argument and that the hot tempered chef responded impulsively.

I gave the cashier a warning and suspended the chef for one day without pay.   On being alone with him, he challenged me in this manner:

"You want to get rid of me." I denied this and reminded him that he was good at his job, and a capable night chef is hard to find.   I also asked him if there was anyone in kitchen who would tell me that he was easy to work with and cooperative.

"So you don't want me gone? What do you want?" I let him know that to keep his job, all he had to do was to be very nice to everyone from now on.

He listened, he changed and kept his job for many years.

CHAPTER VII

WHAT MAKES A GOOD LEADER ?

Certain characteristics make a good leader. Ask yourself this: who have you followed and respected? Analyze the manager's style leading an effort in which you were involved. Examine what was accomplished, What was your contribution to the total effort and what motivated you?

Sport is the best model to look at. A good manager of any team, in baseball or soccer for example, has to know the specific skills of each player. The next step is to understand how they act and react in various situations, and the energy and discipline displayed.

In business people are often promoted based solely on a technical ability.

Fortunately managerial expertise can be acquired.

My first supervisory position as Personnel Director of an 1800 room union hotel in New York City, started my management career. It was clear to me that I had no real qualifications for the job. My promotion was the result of strong interviewing skills and substantial intuition. For some reason, observing behavior of applicants, helped me to evaluate their suitability for the job and the company. Candidates referred by me and hired, tended to do well and stay with the company.

It was certain that the hotel needed a strong opening team of smart personable people, particularly in the HR function.. The Personnel Department, budgeted to have six people. My aim was to lead a diverse group. Good looks, intelligence and energy are needed in the hotel world. Also dealing with executives and union business agents, the staff had to be flexible, articulate and confident. Smart guys were an asset, but could be a threat to a union type, unless tactful by nature.

It is necessary, to look at the total make up of the team. I wanted intelligent, courteous, well educated people around me. My goal was achieved. Forty plus years have gone by and I still am friendly with one of them, and we occasionally share recruiting assignments.

What did I do right? I asked questions about how to proceed, listened and considered the ideas. As we moved in any direction, it was as one. We were a committed team of savvy people, with different styles and personalities.

The main idea is that everyone knows and shares the mission and philosophy of the operation. Whether I am present or not, people know what to do.

Here are messages that will educate your staff:

- Try to solve a problem, using the best interests of the company as a guide.
- If you make a mistake, tell me. We will correct it and I will take responsibility for the results.
- Let me know how you want your career to progress and I'll help you achieve it.
- Tell me what you enjoy doing, what you want to learn and we'll make it happen.

In return, you should ask for and expect your department to be known for its excellence.

CHAPTER VIII

VISION

Powerful leaders have powerful vision, A great example: Winston Churchill, England's Prime Minister stood alone against the Third Reich. One small country – one man with great oratorical skill against a larger country whose leader's rhetoric was also a dynamic feature of his success.

Churchill envisioned the support of the United States if not the free world. He spoke to the British population with fire and enthusiasm. He envisioned the defeat of Germany. Hitler's vision was of World domination by an Aryan race. These were two amazing leaders.

This an example on a grand scale.

You need to envision a future that matches your organization and your department's objectives. What have you been put in charge of and why? Approach your immediate boss and ask some questions.

> **Define for me what is success for this project (or department)?**
>
> **What was the main reason I was selected for this position?**
>
> **Was there anyone else in the department expecting to be in charge?**

As the person in charge of setting up Personnel Offices for several opening hotels, my mission simply stated was "Get and keep the best people". Leading my staff to that purpose, meant sharing with them exactly how I planned to do it, breaking up the goals into smaller pieces and selecting the best person to deal with interviewing, or recording keeping, or benefits, or training and employee relations.

Depending on the size of the property, the General Manager and the Controller and I would create a tentative staffing guide for each area. The Human Resources office tasked with finding 300 employees in total, could plan on seeing at least 3000 people in person and dealing with even more resumes and e-mails. Today that number could be double.

CHAPTER IX

TRUST

Trust is a major component of leadership. Supervisors only interested in their own welfare, never gain or inspire trust.

Whether leading a small or a large group, that group must have faith in your ability to make decisions, understand issues on a broad scale, and be able to use the staff's best talents to the company's and the department's advantage. No playing favorites.

Instead: Think as if you are in charge of a football team, and who you choose for a quarterback. That person has to have real ability.

When you ignore a gifted employee you risk losing them. Intelligent and skilled people at every level, crave a challenge and an opportunity to shine. Provide it and give them credit.

In the far past, women beginning their entry into executive ranks, benefited because of their personality and good looks. Being easy to work with is a distinct asset. Intelligence and follow through guaranteed success.

In the 21st century, things have changed. Man or woman, if you want to succeed, you must be perceived as trustworthy. How is that achieved walking into a new situation? The individual needs to spend time at first listening, asking questions and learning the unspoken rules. It is important to be seen as a team member and collaborator from the beginning. "How may I help in this project? What part of the project is worrisome?"

Never sell a talent you don't have.

How to gain trust:

- Never denigrate or talk about people (anyone) behind their back.
- If you have an issue with anyone, bring it up in a non-threatening way.
- Listen to stated problems and investigate them.
- Give feedback when asked.
- Never try to "one up" anyone.
- If you are faced with not being able to reveal confidential information, say that.
- Do not betray confidences--period. If someone begins to tell you that, "This is between you and me only", let them know up front to be careful because information vital to the well-being of the organization or an individual must be shared, as well as anything illegal.

REMEMBER:
> **Treat everyone with respect and interest.**
> **Honor your commitments.**
> **Share credit for successes.**

Strong leaders have good character. Leaders who win by bullying will lead less gifted people.

HOW TO LOSE TRUST:

> **Say one thing and do another.**
> **Blame others for your mistake.**
> **Gloss over the truth. Lie.**
> **Go back on your word or a promise.**
> **Be spiteful or obviously unkind to your coworkers.**

.

CHAPTER X

COMMUNICATION SKILLS

An organization remains relevant and aware based on the strength of existing dialogues at all levels.

Direct reports: The people reporting to you must be able to speak freely. You need to hear ideas for improvement and growth.

One way to do this is to hold short, no longer than 1 hour meetings. The meeting's agenda can be decided by the person in charge. Set up usually in the morning or just prior to beginning the day's work. The agenda can be shared ahead of time and then divided into three segments: old business, new business and tasks to be accomplished.

Discuss and brainstorm issues with everyone participating. Brain storming demands no criticism and recording of all ideas. Use a giant easel and large pad. Depending on the size of the meeting, allow each person at least two chances to speak. Go around the table.

When this is done, the next step calls for prioritizing. The group studies the issues and ranks them in order of importance with #1 (top number), #2 and #3. Consensus arises as the numbers will easily reveal the group's sense of top priorities. The important issues usually appear as #1 or #2.

The next step is to plan the how and when part. Decide who will do best in each part of the project.

The leader needs to know what tools including time, research, interdepartmental cooperation and skills are required. Ask your staff for this information.   Ask them where they might anticipate resistance or problems.

The message is to talk to your direct reports and make it easy for them to express their ideas.. The people in the trenches need your attention to their details. That means challenging a person if you don't agree with their proposals.

CHAPTER XI

WHY LEADERS FAIL

Good and bad leaders exist. The best leaders always have the ability to listen carefully and respond appropriately.

Leaders need to understand and be able to present the total picture. They need to value the skills of those around them. They need to pick the best talent available.

The most damaging quality in a leader is overwhelming ego and the need to be surrounded by "Yes" men or women. A huge ego means that the individual knows it all and in general feels all powerful and invincible. Leaders must keep informed, flexible and able to evaluate various strategies.

My best boss was above all very smart and an excellent, attentive listener. As the Human Resources function is support to all departments, it is imperative that this department understands what is happening in the organization and can present issues in advance of crisis or problems evolving.

In one of my HR positions, after three years the turnover was almost zero, potential union and employee issues were brought to my attention before problems developed. I had barely 10 hours of work to do in any given week. When there is no turnover, there is almost no interviewing to be done, very little on the benefits roster, and few payroll issues. After leaving, there was no imminent need to replace the position. Accounting could absorb the administrative aspects and competent department heads could effectively manager their staff. This means problems are resolved before they become major concerns.

CONCLUSION

You might enjoy reading the books of Peter Drucker, W. Edwards Deming and Pat Riley. All have wonderful insights on management, motivation and quality issues.

The Leadership Group provides executive search, management consulting, business process improvement, leadership training, and various professional services.

Learn more about us at *www.leadership-goup.com.*

Pat Sherr

www.ingramcontent.com/pod-product-compliance
Lightning Source LLC
Chambersburg PA
CBHW071016200626
45795CB00005B/1832